SANJEEV KAPOOR

Dal-Roti

In association with Alyona Kapoor

Published by
POPULAR PRAKASHAN PVT. LTD.
301, Mahalaxmi Chambers
22, Bhulabhai Desai Road
Mumbai - 400026
for KHANA KHAZANA PUBLICATIONS PVT. LTD.

First Published 2009
Fourth Reprint January 2015

(4316)
ISBN: 978-81-7991-568-4

PRINTED IN INDIA
by Rama Printer
4743/23, Ansari Road, Darya Ganj
New Delhi-110002

Author's Note

A bowl of dal, a couple of rotis and a dollop of pickle on the side - comfort food for maharaja and man-in-the street alike! While people may fantasise about the food of their dreams featuring rich curries and biryanis and exotic vegetables from faraway places, when it comes to the crunch, nothing satisfies the palate and soothes the soul like a simple just-like-mother-made-it dal scooped up with a melt-in-the-mouth piece of roti.

Our mothers and grandmothers knew something that dietitians are now propounding – that legumes and pulses accompanied by whole grains should form the nutritional base of our meals. Legumes, which include lentils, beans and peas, are a good source of calcium, phosphorous, Vitamin B and iron. They are also rich in dietary fibre, which helps lower cholestrol. For vegetarians, legumes are the most important source of protein as they contain more protein than any other plant food. While detractors may claim that the quality of protein is not as good as that provided by fish, chicken and other meats, combined with the proteins in grains they provide a protein which is as good as that provided by any non-vegetarian food.

Which brings us to the importance of rotis in our diets. Especially those made of whole grains, which provide us with dietary fibre, minerals and proteins. They take longer to digest, leaving one with a feeling of fullness which prevents us from overeating. High-fibre foods are believed to decrease the risk of colon cancer and other diseases affecting the gastro-intestinal tract.

Here are some tips for cooking dal and rotis:

- The pressure cooker is the dal's best friend – it is the fastest way to cook dal and also helps to preserve its nutrients.
- Salt and souring agents like lemons, tamarind and tomatoes prevent dal from cooking – they should be added after the dal is cooked.
- Soak legumes overnight and rinse before cooking to reduce the flatulence associated

with eating them. Asafoetida added while cooking also has the same effect.

- Leafy and other vegetables added to *dals* increases their taste and nutritional content.
- Most rotis can be half-cooked in advance and re-cooked just in time. Cool rotis and layer between sheets of greaseproof paper till ready to heat. If planning to freeze rotis, wrap them in foil.
- Place rolled out puris in the refrigerator for ten minutes before frying. They will consume less oil and be crisper.
- Use a kitchen towel to wipe off residual flour that accumulates on the *tawa* after frying two or three rotis.
- To reheat rotis in a microwave oven, wrap them in a paper or cloth napkin and place in the microwave with a bowl of water. The steam will prevent the rotis from drying out.

Happy Cooking!

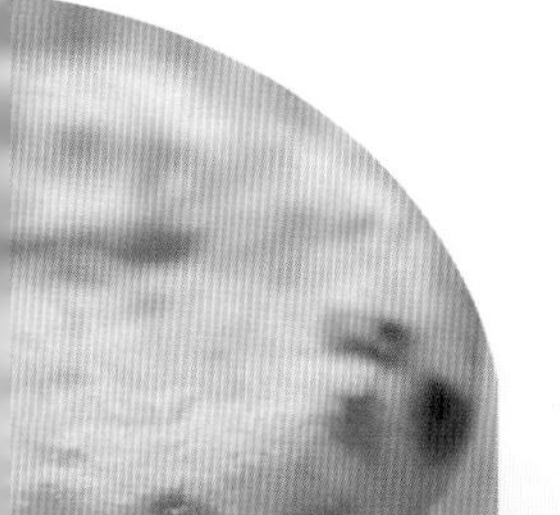

Contents

DAL

ROTI

Char Dal Ka Dalcha

Dal

Ingredients

¼ cup split Bengal gram (*chana dal*)
2 tablespoons split red lentils (*masoor dal*)
¼ cup split pigeon peas (*arhar/toovar dal*)
2 tablespoons split green gram (*moong dal*)
1 teaspoon turmeric powder
1½ teaspoons red chilli powder
salt to taste
1 inch ginger
400 grams bottle gourd (*lauki*)
1 lemon-sized ball tamarind
3 tablespoons oil
2 medium onions, finely sliced
5-6 green chillies, slit
2 tablespoons *desi ghee*
1 teaspoon cumin seeds
5-6 dried red chillies, broken in half
12-15 curry leaves
6-8 garlic cloves, finely chopped

1 Wash and soak the *dals* in plenty of water for at least half an hour. Drain and add half a teaspoon turmeric powder, half a teaspoon red chilli powder, salt and four cups of water. Pressure-cook for four to five minutes, or till completely cooked.

2 Grind ginger to a fine paste. Peel *lauki*, scoop out seeds and cut into one-inch pieces. Soak tamarind in one cup of warm water for half an hour; squeeze out pulp, strain and set aside.

3 Heat oil in a pan; add sliced onions and sauté till light brown. Add ginger paste, the remaining red chilli and turmeric powders and slit green chillies. Sauté for a few minutes and add *lauki*.

4 Sauté for three to four minutes and add the cooked *dals*. Cook, covered, on medium heat for about ten minutes, or till the *lauki* is tender. Add tamarind pulp and half a cup of water; cook over medium heat for four to five minutes, stirring occasionally. Lower heat and simmer for another five minutes.

5 Heat *ghee* in a small pan; add cumin seeds and when they begin to change colour, add red chillies and curry leaves. Sauté for a few seconds; add chopped garlic and sauté till light brown.

6 Pour the sizzling spices over the *dal* and immediately cover the pan with a lid to trap the flavours. Serve hot.

Dahi Lal Masoor

Ingredients

1 cup split red lentils (*masoor dal*)
2 tablespoons yogurt, whisked
salt to taste
½ teaspoon red chilli powder
¼ teaspoon turmeric powder
1 medium onion, sliced
1 tablespoon *ghee*
½ teaspoon cumin seeds
4 garlic cloves, chopped
¼ teaspoon asafoetida (*hing*)

1. Wash *dal* in several changes of water; soak in three cups of water for one hour; drain.

2. Place the *dal* with two-and-half cups of water, salt, red chilli powder, turmeric powder and sliced onions in a pressure cooker and cook until pressure is released once (one whistle).

3. Lower heat and simmer for five minutes. Take the cooker off the heat and allow pressure to reduce completely before removing the lid.

4. Heat *ghee* in a pan; add cumin seeds and garlic. When the seeds begin to change colour, add asafoetida and immediately pour the sizzling spices over the *dal*.

5. Remove from heat and stir in the whisked yogurt. Serve hot.

Kale Vatanyachi Amti

Ingredients

1½ cups black peas (*kale vatane*), soaked overnight

3 medium onions

2 tablespoons oil

2 tablespoons grated dried coconut (*khopra*)

4-5 garlic cloves

½ cup grated fresh coconut

a pinch of asafoetida (*hing*)

½ teaspoon turmeric powder

1 tablespoon red chilli powder

1 teaspoon cumin powder

1 teaspoon coriander powder

salt to taste

4 pieces of *kokum*

1 teaspoon grated jaggery (optional)

1 teaspoon *garam masala* powder

a few sprigs of fresh coriander leaves, chopped

1 Slice one onion and finely chop the other two. Heat one tablespoon of oil and sauté sliced onion till pink. Add grated dried coconut and sauté till lightly coloured. Add garlic and sauté for a few seconds.

2 Cool and grind the mixture with a little water to a fine paste. Grind three-fourth of the grated fresh coconut to a fine paste separately.

3 Heat remaining oil in a pan. Add asafoetida and finely chopped onions and sauté on high heat till golden brown.

4 Add turmeric powder, red chilli powder, cumin powder, coriander powder and soaked peas and stir well to mix.

5 Add three cups of hot water and salt to taste and bring to a boil. Cover and cook over low heat till the peas are soft.

6 Add *kokum*, coconut-onion paste and fresh coconut paste. Mix well and simmer for two to three minutes.

7 Add the jaggery and *garam masala* powder and mix well.

8 Stir in the chopped coriander leaves.

9 Garnish with the remaining grated coconut and serve hot with rice *wade* (page 72).

Dhuli Urad Dal

Ingredients

2 cups split black gram (*dhuli urad dal*)
10-12 *urad dal wadi*
2 tablespoons oil + for deep-frying
a pinch of asafoetida (*hing*)
1 teaspoon cumin seeds
salt to taste
¼ teaspoon turmeric powder
½ teaspoon red chilli powder
1 medium tomato, chopped
½ teaspoon lemon juice
1 inch ginger, cut into thin strips

1. Soak *urad dal* in four cups of water for one hour. Drain.

2. Heat oil in a *kadai* and deep-fry the *urad dal wadis* till golden. Drain on absorbent paper.

3. Heat two tablespoons of oil in a pan; add asafoetida and cumin seeds. When the cumin seeds begin to change colour, stir in the *urad dal*.

4. Add salt, turmeric powder, red chilli powder and tomato, and sauté for one minute. Add four-and-a-half cups of water, and when it comes to a boil, lower heat and cook till the *dal* is soft.

5. Stir in the fried *wadis* and lemon juice. Serve hot, garnished with ginger strips.

Dal Dhokli

Ingredients

¾ cup split pigeon peas (*arhar/toovar dal*)
¾ cup wholewheat flour (*atta*)
2 tablespoons gram flour (*besan*)
salt to taste
¾ teaspoon turmeric powder
¾ teaspoon red chilli powder
2 pinches asafoetida (*hing*)
½ tablespoon oil
1½ tablespoons peanuts
1 tablespoon *ghee*
¼ teaspoon mustard seeds
½ teaspoon cumin seeds
4 garlic cloves, peeled and finely chopped
4 curry leaves
3 pieces of *kokum*
1½ teaspoons grated jaggery
2 tablespoons fresh coriander leaves, finely chopped

1 Wash *dal* in several changes of water; soak in two cups of water for half an hour.

2 Mix wholewheat flour and gram flour. Add salt, one-fourth teaspoon turmeric powder, red chilli powder, a pinch of asafoetida, oil and enough water to make

a stiff dough. Roll the dough out into thin *rotis* and cut into desired shapes.

3 Boil the *dal* with one-and-a-half cups of water. When the *dal* is half-cooked, add peanuts and remaining turmeric powder.

4 Heat *ghee* in a pan; add mustard seeds, cumin seeds, a pinch of asafoetida, garlic and curry leaves and sauté for a few seconds. Pour the sizzling spices into the *dal*.

5 Add two cups of water and *kokum* to the *dal* and bring to a boil; stir in the jaggery.

6 Add the strips of dough and cook, stirring occasionally, so that the pieces of dough do not stick to the bottom of the pan.

7 Adjust salt and serve hot, garnished with chopped coriander leaves.

Dal Makhani

Ingredients

½ cup whole black gram (*sabut urad*), soaked
2 tablespoons red kidney beans (*rajma*), soaked
salt to taste
1 teaspoon red chilli powder
2 inches ginger, chopped
1 tablespoon oil
3 tablespoons butter
1 teaspoon cumin seeds
1 large onion, chopped
6 garlic cloves, chopped
2 medium tomatoes, chopped
1 teaspoon *garam masala* powder
½ cup fresh cream

1 Cook the soaked lentils and beans in three cups of water with salt, red chilli powder and half the ginger till cooked and soft.

2 Heat oil and butter in a thick-bottomed pan. Add cumin seeds; when the seeds change colour, add onion and fry till golden brown.

3 Add the remaining ginger, garlic and tomatoes. Sauté till tomatoes are pulpy and the fat begins to separate. Add boiled lentils and beans.

4 Add half a cup of water and *garam masala* powder; bring to a boil, lower heat and simmer for fifteen minutes.

5 Stir in the fresh cream and simmer for another five minutes.

6 Serve hot with *naan* (page 84) or *parantha.*

CHEF'S TIP

Reheated Dal Makhani tastes just as good (even better!) the following day. I like it cold too! The *paranthas*, however, should be piping hot.

Mixed Kali Dal

Ingredients

¾ cup whole black gram (*sabut urad*)
3 tablespoons red kidney beans (*rajma*)
3 tablespoons split Bengal gram (*chana dal*)
3 one-inch pieces ginger
7-8 garlic cloves
salt to taste
2 teaspoons red chilli powder
2 tablespoons pure *ghee*
3 tablespoons butter
1 teaspoon cumin seeds
1 medium onion, chopped
3 dried red chillies, broken in half
1 cup tomato purée
1 teaspoon *garam masala* powder
2 tablespoons fresh coriander leaves, chopped
¼ cup fresh cream (*malai*)

1 Wash *sabut urad*, *rajma* and *chana dal* together in several changes of water. Soak in four cups of water for eight hours. Cut two pieces of ginger into fine strips and grind the remaining piece with garlic to a fine paste.

2 Place the soaked *dals* in a pressure cooker with ginger strips, salt, red chilli powder and three cups of water. Cook over high heat till pressure is released twice (two whistles). Lower heat and cook for about fifteen minutes.

3 Heat *ghee* and butter in a small pan. Add cumin seeds and onion and sauté for a few minutes. Add red chillies and ginger-garlic paste and sauté for two minutes. Stir in the tomato purée.

4 Add *garam masala* powder and the spice mixture to the cooked *dals* and mash the *dals* slightly with the back of a spoon.

5 Add one cup of water and bring to a boil; lower heat and simmer for two minutes. Stir in the coriander leaves and cream and serve piping hot.

CHEF'S TIP

In this recipe, the traditional "*mah ki dal*" is enriched by the addition of *rajma* and *chana dal.*

Sookhi Dal Amritsari

Ingredients

1 cup skinless split black gram (*dhuli urad dal*), soaked

salt to taste

½ teaspoon turmeric powder

3 one-inch pieces ginger, cut into thin strips

4 tablespoons oil

a pinch of asafoetida (*hing*)

1½ teaspoons cumin seeds

2 medium onions, chopped

4-5 green chillies, chopped

3 medium tomatoes, chopped

1 teaspoon red chilli powder

¾ teaspoon *garam masala* powder

2 tablespoons fresh coriander leaves, chopped

4 teaspoons lemon juice

1. Put the *dal*, three cups of water, salt, turmeric powder and half the ginger into a deep pan. Bring the mixture to a boil, lower heat and cook till just done.
2. Heat the oil in a separate pan; add asafoetida, cumin seeds and onions. Sauté till the onions turn light pink.

3 Add the remaining ginger, green chillies and tomatoes and sauté for a few seconds. Add the red chilli powder and sauté till the oil separates.

4 Strain the *dal* and add to the *masala*; stir well. Stir in the salt, *garam masala* powder, coriander leaves and lemon juice. Cook for two more minutes and serve hot.

CHEF'S TIP

Salt is added while cooking the *dal* to ensure it retains its texture and to prevent it from overcooking.

Sprouted Moong Kadhi

Ingredients

¾ cup green gram (*moong*), sprouted
1 cup yogurt
¼ cup gram flour (*besan*)
1 tablespoon grated jaggery
1 inch ginger, finely chopped
salt to taste
2 tablespoons oil
½ teaspoon cumin seeds
½ teaspoon fenugreek seeds (*methi dana*)
¼ teaspoon asafoetida (*hing*)
7-8 curry leaves
4 dried red chillies, broken in half
6-8 black peppercorns, crushed

1 Cook sprouted *moong* in two cups of water for five minutes. Drain.

2 Whisk together yogurt and gram flour till smooth. Stir in jaggery, ginger and two cups of water.

3 Transfer yogurt mixture to a deep pan and cook over medium heat, stirring continuously, till the mixture thickens. Add cooked *moong* and cook for another three to four minutes. Add salt.

4 Heat oil in a small pan; add cumin seeds, fenugreek seeds, asafoetida and curry leaves. When the seeds begin to change colour, add red chillies and crushed peppercorns. Pour over the *kadhi*.

Gujarati Kadhi

Ingredients

¼ cup gram flour (*besan*)
2 cups yogurt
1 lemon-sized piece jaggery
2 green chillies, finely chopped
salt to taste
2 tablespoons oil
½ teaspoon mustard seeds
½ teaspoon cumin seeds
8-10 curry leaves
2 dried red chillies
3-4 cloves
1 inch cinnamon
⅛ teaspoon asafoetida (*hing*)

1 Whisk *besan* and yogurt together till smooth. Add four cups of water and mix well.

2 Grate jaggery and add to yogurt mixture with green chillies.

3 Transfer the mixture to a pan and cook, stirring continuously, till the *kadhi* is moderately thick. Add salt to taste.

4 Heat oil in a small pan; add mustard seeds, cumin seeds, curry leaves, red chillies, cloves, cinnamon and asafoetida. When the seeds begin to splutter, pour over the *kadhi* and stir well. Serve hot.

Varan

Ingredients

½ cup split pigeon peas (*arhar/toovar dal*)
¼ tsp turmeric power
salt to taste
2 teaspoons pure *ghee*
a pinch of asafoetida (*hing*)
½ teaspoon cumin seeds

1. Soak *dal* for half an hour in one cup of water.
2. Bring *dal*, three cups of water, salt and turmeric powder to a boil. Cook till the *dal* is soft. Mash thoroughly.
3. Heat the *ghee* in a pan. Add asafoetida and cumin seeds. When the cumin seeds change colour, pour over the mashed *dal* and cover the pan immediately to trap the flavours.
4. Serve hot

Cholar Dal

Ingredients

1 cup split Bengal gram (*chana dal*)
3 tablespoons *ghee*
¼ coconut, cut into ¼-inch pieces
½ teaspoon turmeric powder
salt to taste
1 teaspoon sugar
3 cloves
1 inch cinnamon
1 black cardamom
½ teaspoon cumin seeds
2 bay leaves
2 dried red chillies
2 green chillies, slit
1 teaspoon ginger paste
1 teaspoon raisins (*kishmish*)

1 Wash and soak the *dal* for one hour. Drain and pressure-cook with three cups of water till just done.

2 Heat two tablespoons of *ghee* in a pan and fry coconut pieces till golden. Drain.

3 Add turmeric powder, salt and sugar to the *dal* and simmer over low heat till most of the water is absorbed and the *dal* is thick.

4 Heat the remaining *ghee* in a separate pan. Add cloves, cinnamon, black

cardamom, cumin seeds, bay leaves, red chillies and green chillies and sauté for two minutes. Pour the spices into the simmering *dal*.

5 Stir in the ginger paste, fried coconut and raisins and simmer for five more minutes.

6 Serve hot with *luchis* (page 67).

CHEF'S TIP

While the traditional recipe for *Cholar Dal* calls for adding pieces of coconut, which adds a unique texture to the dish, you may add grated coconut instead.

Tomato Paruppu Rasam

Ingredients

4 tablespoons split pigeon peas (*arhar/toovar dal*)
½ lemon-sized tamarind ball
¼ cup fresh coriander leaves, chopped
1½ teaspoons *rasam* powder
¼ teaspoon asafoetida (*hing*)
salt to taste
10-12 curry leaves
2 medium tomatoes, chopped
4 tablespoons pure *ghee*
½ teaspoon mustard seeds
2 dried red chillies

1. Wash *dal* in several changes of water; drain and cook in two cups of water until soft. Strain and mash well. Reserve the strained cooking liquid.

2. Soak tamarind in one cup of warm water; squeeze out pulp, strain and reserve.

3. Reserve some coriander leaves for garnishing. Mix tamarind pulp with remaining chopped coriander, *rasam* powder, asafoetida, salt and half the curry leaves. Bring to a boil, lower heat and simmer for two to three minutes.

4 Add chopped tomatoes and the reserved cooking liquid. Simmer for four to five minutes and stir in the mashed *dal*. Stir well and cook for one minute more.

5 Remove from heat and sprinkle the reserved chopped coriander leaves.

6 Heat pure *ghee* in a small pan; add mustard seeds and sauté till they begin to splutter. Add red chillies and remaining curry leaves and stir well. Pour the sizzling spices over the *rasam* and cover immediately to trap the flavours. Serve hot.

CHEF'S TIP

To serve *rasam* as an appetiser, strain and pour into small glasses, garnished with a slice of lemon. Traditionally, *rasams* are cooked in a pan made from a special alloy, which gives the *rasam* its unique flavour.

Paruppu Urundai Kozhambu

Dal

Ingredients

1 cup split pigeon peas (*arhar/toovar dal*)
¼ cup split Bengal gram (*chana dal*)
8 dried red chillies
5 tablespoons oil
a pinch of asafoetida (*hing*)
1 teaspoon mustard seeds
1 medium onion, chopped
2 green chillies, chopped
¼ cup grated fresh coconut
salt to taste
20 curry leaves
¼ cup fresh coriander leaves, chopped
1 tablespoon rice flour
½ teaspoon fenugreek seeds (*methi dana*)
1½ teaspoons *sambhar* powder
1½ tablespoons tamarind pulp

1. Soak *arhar* and *chana dals* in four cups of water for half an hour. Drain and crush with six red chillies.

2. Heat half the oil in a pan. Add asafoetida, half the mustard seeds, onion and green chillies, and sauté for a few minutes.

3 Stir in the coconut and the crushed *dals* and sauté for a while. Add salt and mix. Cook for five to eight minutes. Cool.

4 Chop half the curry leaves, and add to the *dal* mixture with half the coriander leaves and rice flour and mix well. Shape into small balls (*koftas*).

5 Heat remaining oil in a pan. Break the remaining red chillies into pieces and add to the pan with remaining mustard seeds, fenugreek seeds, remaining curry leaves, *sambhar* powder and one-and-a-half cups of water. Mix well. When the mixture comes to a boil, add salt and the *koftas*.

6 Add tamarind pulp, remaining coriander leaves and stir to mix. Cover and cook over medium heat for about ten minutes till the gravy is thick and the *koftas* are cooked. Serve hot.

Punjabi Kadhi

Ingredients

Pakoras

¾ cup gram flour (*besan*)

1 medium onion, finely chopped

½ bunch (125 grams) fenugreek leaves (*methi*), chopped

1 inch ginger, grated

1 teaspoon carom seeds (*ajwain*)

1 teaspoon red chilli powder

¼ teaspoon baking powder

salt to taste

oil for deep-frying

Kadhi

1 cup yogurt

¼ cup gram flour (*besan*)

1 teaspoon turmeric powder

salt to taste

2 tablespoons oil

½ teaspoon fenugreek seeds (*methi dana*)

½ teaspoon cumin seeds

2 dried red chillies, broken in half

6 black peppercorns

1 medium onion, sliced (optional)

½ inch ginger, chopped

1 teaspoon red chilli powder

1. Mix all the ingredients for the *pakoras*, except oil, with half a cup of water.

2. Heat oil in a *kadai*; drop small portions of the *besan* mixture into the hot oil and deep-fry till golden brown. Drain on absorbent paper.

3. For the *kadhi*, whisk yogurt well with the *besan* till smooth. Add turmeric powder, salt and three cups of water.

4. Heat oil in a *kadai*; add fenugreek seeds, cumin seeds, red chillies and peppercorns. Sauté for half a minute.

5. Add sliced onion and chopped ginger and sauté for one minute. Stir in the yogurt mixture, bring to a boil, lower heat and simmer for about fifteen minutes, stirring occasionally.

6. Add red chilli powder and fried *pakoras* and continue to simmer for four to five minutes. Serve hot.

Sultani Dal

Ingredients

½ cup split pigeon peas (*arhar/toovar dal*)
½ cup fresh cream
½ cup yogurt
6 cloves
10 green cardamoms, peeled
salt to taste
1 teaspoon red chilli powder
1 betel leaf
a piece of charcoal
1 tablespoon *ghee*
1 teaspoon cumin seeds
8 garlic cloves, cut into thin slivers
2 green chillies, finely chopped
5-6 sprigs fresh mint leaves

1. Wash the *dal* in several changes of water; soak *dal* for ten minutes.
2. Mix together fresh cream and yogurt and pass the mixture through a piece of muslin. Set aside in a cool place. Grind cloves and green cardamoms together with a little water to a smooth paste.
3. Boil *dal* with salt, red chilli powder and four cups of water. Cover and cook over low heat till *dal* is soft. Drain.

4 Return *dal* to pan and mash thoroughly with the back of a ladle till smooth.

5 Place the betel leaf on the *dal* and put a small piece of burning charcoal on it. Pour one teaspoon of *ghee* over the coal and immediately cover the pan. Leave covered for ten minutes to flavour the dish with the smoke (*dhungar*). Remove charcoal and betel leaf and discard.

6 Stir in the yogurt-cream mixture and clove-cardamom paste. Cover and simmer for five minutes.

7 Heat the remaining *ghee* in a small seasoning (*tadka*) pan; add cumin seeds and garlic. When the garlic turns pink, pour into the *dal* and cover immediately.

8 Uncover the pan, stir lightly, and serve hot, garnished with green chillies and mint leaves.

Rajasthani Panchmel Dal

Ingredients

¼ cup split Bengal gram (*chana dal*)
¼ cup whole green gram (*sabut moong*)
¼ cup split black gram (*dhuli urad dal*)
¼ cup split pigeon peas (*arhar/toovar dal*)
¼ cup red lentils (*masoor*)
½ teaspoon turmeric powder
salt to taste
1 inch ginger, chopped
2 green chillies, chopped
3 tablespoons oil
a pinch of asafoetida (*hing*)
½ teaspoon cumin seeds
4-5 cloves
2 dried red chillies, broken in half
1 teaspoon cumin powder
1 teaspoon coriander powder
½ teaspoon red chilli powder
2 medium tomatoes, chopped
½ teaspoon *garam masala* powder
2 tablespoons coriander leaves, chopped

1 Wash all the pulses in several changes of water. Soak for at least two hours. Drain and boil in enough water, with turmeric powder and salt till cooked.

2 Grind ginger and green chillies to a paste.

3 Heat oil in a pan; add asafoetida, cumin seeds, cloves and red chillies. When the cumin seeds begin to change colour, add ginger-green chilli paste and sauté for a few seconds.

4 Stir in the cumin powder, coriander powder and red chilli powder. Add the tomatoes and cook till the oil separates. Add cooked lentils and additional water if required.

5 Cook for ten minutes, stirring occasionally. Add *garam masala* powder and coriander leaves serve hot.

Rajma Masala

Ingredients

1 cup kidney beans (*rajma*)
¼ teaspoon soda bicarbonate
2 medium onions, chopped
7-8 garlic cloves, chopped
1 inch ginger, chopped
4 tablespoons oil
2-3 green chillies, chopped
1 teaspoon red chilli powder
2 teaspoons coriander powder
1 teaspoon cumin powder
4 medium tomatoes, puréed
salt to taste
1½ teaspoons *garam masala* powder
2 tablespoons fresh coriander leaves, chopped

1 Soak the kidney beans overnight in four cups of water to which soda bicarbonate has been added. Drain and rinse in fresh water.

2 Cook *rajma* with five cups of water in a pressure cooker till pressure is released four or five times (four or five whistles).

3 Grind onions, garlic and ginger to a smooth paste.

4 Heat oil in a *kadai*; add ground paste and chopped green chillies and sauté till pale gold. Add red chilli powder, coriander powder and cumin powder. Sauté for two minutes.

5 Stir in the tomato purée and sauté till the oil separates.

6 Stir in the kidney beans with two cups of water and salt; bring to a boil, cover and lower the heat. Simmer for about ten minutes.

7 Stir in *garam masala* powder. Garnish with coriander leaves and serve hot.

Ras No Fajeto

Ingredients

½ cup ripe mango pulp
2¼ tablespoons gram flour (*besan*)
¼ teaspoon turmeric powder
salt to taste
2¼ cups sour buttermilk
1½ tablespoons oil
a pinch of asafoetida (*hing*)
½ teaspoon cumin seeds
6 curry leaves
2 green chillies, chopped
¾ tablespoon jaggery

1. Put the mango pulp into a bowl with the gram flour, turmeric powder and salt and whisk till smooth.
2. Add buttermilk and mix well.
3. Heat oil in a pan; add asafoetida, cumin seeds, curry leaves and green chillies and sauté for one minute. Add the mango mixture and jaggery and mix again.
4. Add enough water to get the desired consistency.
5. Bring the mixture to a boil, lower heat and simmer for five minutes.
6. Serve hot with steamed rice or *roti*.

Sambhar

Ingredients

½ cup split pigeon peas (*arhar/toovar dal*)
¼ teaspoon turmeric powder
4 tablespoons sesame (*til*) oil
1 lemon-sized ball tamarind
½ teaspoon mustard seeds
4 dried red chillies
½ teaspoon fenugreek seeds (*methi dana*), optional
¼ teaspoon asafoetida (*hing*)
4 green chillies, slit
10-12 curry leaves
2 drumsticks (*saijan ki phalli*), cut into 2 ½ -inch pieces
1½ teaspoons *sambhar* powder
salt to taste
1 teaspoon rice flour
¼ cup fresh coriander leaves, chopped

1 Wash the *dal* and pressure-cook in two-and-a-half cups of water with turmeric powder and one teaspoon of oil. Mash the cooked *dal* lightly with a wooden spoon.

2 Soak tamarind in one cup of warm water; squeeze out pulp and strain.

3 Heat oil in a thick-bottomed pan; add mustard seeds, and sauté till they begin to splutter. Add red chillies, fenugreek seeds and asafoetida.

4 Add slit green chillies, curry leaves and drumsticks, and cook over medium heat, stirring continuously for a few minutes.

5 Stir in the tamarind pulp, *sambhar* powder, salt and one cup of water.

6 Lower heat and simmer for six to eight minutes, or till drumsticks are cooked. Add boiled *dal* and simmer for two or three minutes.

7 Mix rice flour and a quarter cup of water and stir into the *sambhar*. Cook for two or three minutes more, stirring occasionally.

8 Sprinkle chopped coriander leaves over the *dal* and serve hot.

CHEF'S TIP

You can add vegetables such as white radish, ladies' fingers, pumpkin, brinjals, *sambhar* onions etc., either individually or in any combination. In South India, each family has its own recipe for *sambhar*.

Tur Dal Ross

Ingredients

½ cup split pigeon peas (*arhar/toovar dal*)
1 drumstick (*saijan ki phalli*) cut into 2-inch pieces
5 *tirphal*, pitted
¼ cup grated fresh coconut
¾ teaspoon red chilli powder
a pinch of turmeric powder
½ tablespoon tamarind pulp
salt to taste
½ teaspoon grated jaggery

1 Soak *dal* in one-and-a-half cups of water for half an hour. Drain and cook in one-and-a-half cups of water till completely cooked. Whisk well till smooth.

2 Cook drumstick in one cup of water till tender. Drain.

3 Grind *tirphal* in one-fourth cup of water. Strain and reserve the water.

4 Grind the coconut, red chilli powder, turmeric powder and tamarind pulp with a little water to a smooth paste.

5 Add the ground *masala*, drumstick, and *tirphal* water to the whisked *dal* and mix well. Stir in one cup of water, salt and jaggery; bring the mixture to a boil, lower heat and simmer for three to four minutes. Serve hot

Sindhi Kadhi

Ingredients

½ cup split pigeon peas (*arhar/toovar dal*)
3 medium tomatoes, halved
3 tablespoons oil
6-8 small ladies' fingers (*bhindi*), slit
2-3 green chillies, slit
70 grams cluster beans (*gwar*)
¾ teaspoon cumin seeds
¼ teaspoon fenugreek seeds (*methi dana*)
a pinch of asafoetida (*hing*), optional
3 tablespoons gram flour (*besan*)
salt to taste
1 teaspoon red chilli powder
¼ teaspoon turmeric powder
2 tablespoons tamarind pulp
7-8 curry leaves

1 Wash and soak *dal* in two cups of water for about half an hour. Drain.

2 Cook *dal* in a pressure cooker with halved tomatoes and two cups of water for ten minutes or till soft.

3 Mash the *dal* well and pass through a strainer, pressing the *dal* through with the back of a ladle.

4 Heat one tablespoon of oil in a pan; add ladies' fingers and sauté for a few

minutes. Add slit green chillies and *gwar* and continue to sauté for two to three minutes. Set aside.

5 Heat one tablespoon of oil in a heavy-bottomed pan; add half a teaspoon of cumin seeds, the fenugreek seeds and asafoetida.

6 When the cumin seeds begin to change colour, add *besan* and sauté for about five minutes. Gradually add three cups of water, stirring continuously to prevent lumps from forming.

7 Stir in the mashed *dal*, salt, red chilli powder and turmeric powder. Add a little water to the tamarind pulp and stir it into the *kadhi*. Add the sautéed vegetables and mix well.

8 In a separate pan, heat the remaining oil; add the remaining cumin seeds and curry leaves. When the cumin seeds change colour pour over the *kadhi*. Serve hot.

Amritsari Aloo Kulcha

Ingredients

First dough

2 cups refined flour (*maida*)

½ teaspoon baking powder

¼ teaspoon soda bicarbonate

½ teaspoon salt

1 tablespoon yogurt

½ egg

½ cup milk

1 teaspoon sugar

1 tablespoon oil

Second dough

2 cups refined flour (*maida*)

salt to taste

4 tablespoons butter

½ cup milk

Stuffing

2 medium potatoes, boiled, peeled and grated

½ medium onion, chopped

salt to taste

2 green chillies, chopped

2 teaspoons red chilli powder

1 tablespoon cumin powder

1 teaspoon pomegranate seeds (*anardana*)

2 tablespoons fresh coriander leaves, chopped

1. To make the first dough, sift flour with baking powder, soda bicarbonate and salt. Add yogurt, egg, milk, sugar and a little water. Knead well to make a medium soft dough.

2. Add a little oil and knead again. Cover with a damp cloth and rest the dough for one hour. Knead the dough once again and divide into eight equal portions.

3. For the second dough, sift refined flour with salt. Rub in the butter with your fingertips till the mixture resembles coarse crumbs. Gradually mix in the milk and knead to make a soft smooth dough. Cover with a damp cloth and rest the dough for ten minutes.

4. Knead the dough once again and divide it into eight equal portions and shape into smooth balls. Cover with a damp cloth and set aside for another ten minutes.

5. For the stuffing, mix together potatoes, onion, salt, green chillies, red chilli powder, cumin powder, *anardana* and coriander leaves.

6. Divide the potato mixture into eight equal portions.

7. Flatten a portion of the first dough, place a portion of the potato mixture in the centre and fold the dough over to form a ball.

8 Flatten a portion of the second dough and place the stuffed ball in the centre and roll into a ball. Place on a lightly-floured surface and roll out gently into a circle.

9 Heat a pressure cooker. Dip your fingers in a little water and moisten one side of the *kulcha*. Gently press the moistened side of the *kulcha* onto the inner wall of the pressure cooker, making sure the *kulcha* is moist enough to stick to the cooker.

10 Place the cooker upside down over an open flame to make a kind of *tandoor*. Cook over high heat for two to three minutes, lower heat and cook for two to three minutes more.

11 Turn the cooker upright and gently peel the *kulcha* away from the cooker wall.

12 Brush the hot *kulcha* with butter and serve immediately.

13 You can also cook *kulchas* in a preheated oven at 220°C/425°F/Gas Mark 7 for about eight minutes.

Bajre Ki Roti With Banana Stuffing

Ingredients

Dough

¾ cup *bajra* flour

¼ cup refined flour (*maida*)

salt to taste

1 tablespoon oil + for shallow-frying

roasted sesame seeds (*til*)

Filling

3 medium unripe *Rajeri* bananas

salt to taste

2 teaspoons green chilli paste

1 teaspoon sugar

2 teaspoons lemon juice

1 tablespoon fresh coriander leaves, chopped

1 To make the filling, steam the unpeeled bananas; peel and mash while still hot. Add salt, green chilli paste, sugar, lemon juice and coriander leaves. Mix well till smooth.

2 To make the dough, put the *bajra* flour, refined flour and salt into a bowl and mix well. Add one tablespoon of oil and enough water and knead into a soft dough. Divide into eight equal *pedhas*.

3 Sprinkle some refined flour on the worktop, place a *pedha* on it and gently spread it out with your fingers, making sure that the outer edges are thinner than the centre. Place a portion of the stuffing in the centre and gather the edges together and roll out once again into a *pedha*.

4 Lightly press one side of the *pedha* into the roasted sesame seeds. Roll in refined flour and gently flatten the *pedha* with your fingers to make as thin a *roti* as you can. You need not use a rolling pin.

5 Heat a *tawa* and place the *roti* on it. When one side is lightly browned, turn over and cook the other side. Drizzle some oil all around and continue to cook till both sides are light golden brown. Serve hot.

CHEF'S TIP

Refined flour is used in the dough because it helps to bind the *bajra* flour into a dough.

Makki Di Roti

Ingredients

1½ cups cornmeal (*makai ka atta*)
¼ cup wholewheat flour (*atta*), optional
salt to taste
fresh home-made white butter

1 Add salt and wholewheat flour to the cornmeal and mix well. Add warm water and knead to make a medium soft dough. Divide into eight equal portions and shape into balls.

2 Pat each ball between moistened palms into a moderately thick *roti*. Alternatively, roll out each ball between the folds of a greased plastic sheet.

3 Heat a *tawa* and place a *roti* on it. Cook over medium heat till one side is half-done. Turn over and spread some white butter over the surface. Turn over and spread some more butter on the other side. Cook till both sides are golden brown.

4 Serve hot with a dollop of white butter.

Jawari Bhakri

Ingredients

2 tablespoons *jawari* flour
salt to taste
½ cup fresh white butter

1 Mix together the *jawari* flour and salt.

2 Add enough water to make a soft dough; knead well.

3 Divide dough into eight equal portions. Shape each portion into a round ball. Roll out each portion of dough into a thin round.

4 Heat a *tawa* till moderately hot. Cook each *bhakri* on the *tawa* until one side is cooked.

5 Sprinkle a little water on the *bhakri*, turn over and cook the other side till done.

6 Serve hot with a dollop of fresh white butter.

Luchi

Ingredients

2 cups refined flour (*maida*)
1 cup water (approximately)
oil for deep-frying
1 teaspoon salt
1 tablespoon *ghee*

1. Sift flour with salt. Add *ghee* and enough water to make a soft dough. Cover with a damp cloth and set aside for half an hour.

2. Divide the dough into twenty equal portions and shape into small balls.

3. Roll each ball into a three-inch round *luchi*.

4. Heat oil in a *kadai* and deep-fry the *luchis* till puffed up and a pale cream colour.

5. Serve immediately.

Baby Bajra Roti

Ingredients

2 cups *bajra* flour
salt to taste
4 tablespoons white butter (optional)

1. Heat two or three cups of water in a pan till lukewarm. Place *tawa* over a low heat.

2. Combine one-fourth of the *bajra* flour and salt to taste, and knead with lukewarm water to make a semi-hard dough. Roll into a ball.

3. Wet your hands and pat the ball of dough into a *roti*.

4. Heat a *tawa* till moderately hot and place the *roti* on it. Cook on one side and flip over. Continue cooking till the *roti* puffs up.

5. Remove from heat and serve hot with butter.

6. Repeat the process to make the rest of the *rotis*.

Bhature

Ingredients

2½ cups refined flour (*maida*)
½ teaspoon baking powder
a pinch of soda bicarbonate
1 teaspoon salt
½ cup yogurt
2 teaspoons powdered sugar
2 tablespoons oil + for deep-frying

1. Sift flour, baking powder, soda bicarbonate and salt together.
2. Mix yogurt with sugar; add to the flour with approximately one cup of water, mix well and knead lightly into a soft dough.
3. Rub two tablespoons of oil into the dough. Cover the dough with a damp cloth and set aside for one hour.
4. Divide dough into sixteen equal portions and roll into balls. Cover and leave to ferment for ten minutes.
5. Grease your palms with a little oil and flatten the balls. Roll out into five-inch rounds.
6. Heat oil in a *kadai* and deep-fry *bhature* on high heat till light brown on both sides.

CHEF'S TIP

To make oval *bhature*, stretch the rolled out circles of dough in opposite directions.

Chawal Ka Parantha

Ingredients

1 cup cooked rice
1¼ cups wholewheat flour (*atta*)
1 teaspoon salt + to taste
¼ cup yogurt
2 tablespoons *ghee*
½ teaspoon red chilli powder
½ teaspoon cumin powder
2 green chillies, chopped
1 medium onion, chopped
oil for frying

1. Sift wholewheat flour with one teaspoon of salt. Mix into a soft dough with yogurt, two tablespoons of *ghee* and half a cup of water. Cover with a damp cloth and set aside for half an hour.

2. Mix cooked rice with red chilli powder, cumin powder, chopped green chillies, chopped onion and salt to taste.

3. Knead again and divide into four equal portions. Shape each portion into a ball and press between the palms of your hands to form a *pedha*. Roll out each *pedha* into a three-inch round.

4. Stuff with rice mixture and shape into a thick round *pedha*. Roll out into a seven-inch circle.

5 Heat a *tawa* and place a *parantha* on it. Turn over once and spread some oil on it. Turn over again and spread a little more oil on the other side. Cook till both sides are well cooked.

CHEF'S TIP

You can use leftover rice, which need not be reheated and can be used straight out of the refrigerator.

Rice Wade

Ingredients

2 cups rice flour
2 tablespoons fennel seeds (*saunf*)
1 tablespoon fenugreek seeds (*methi dana*)
salt to taste
1 small onion, grated
oil for deep-frying

1. Boil one-and-a-quarter cups of water with fennel and fenugreek seeds for about five minutes to extract their flavour.

2. Strain and reheat the water. Stir in the salt and rice flour and cook, stirring continuously, till the mixture comes together and leaves the sides of the pan.

3. Transfer the dough to a bowl, add grated onion and mix well.

4. Grease your palms and divide the dough into twelve equal balls. Press each ball of dough between your palms to make a *wada*.

5 Heat oil in a *kadai* and deep-fry the *wadas* till golden brown and cooked. Drain on absorbent paper and serve hot.

CHEF'S TIP

You can also shape the *wadas* on greaseproof paper. Place a ball of dough between two sheets of greased greaseproof paper and flatten it with a rolling pin or your fingers. Remove the top sheet of paper and gently remove the *wada* from the bottom sheet and deep-fry.

Koki

Ingredients

2½ cups wholewheat flour (*atta*)
2 small onions, roughly chopped
salt to taste
2-3 green chillies, finely chopped
2 tablespoons fresh coriander leaves, chopped
1 tablespoon *ghee* + for shallow-frying
4 tablespoons fresh cream (*malai*)

1. Mix together the *atta*, onions, salt, green chillies, coriander leaves, *ghee* and *malai* in a bowl. Add enough water to make a stiff dough. Cover and rest the dough for about fifteen minutes.

2. Divide the dough into eight equal portions, larger in size than that needed to make a *parantha*. Pat with your fingers into a thick round.

3. Heat a *tawa*, place the *koki* on it and cook on both sides. Brush with pure *ghee* and cook till both sides are light golden in colour.

4. Serve hot.

Missi Roti

Ingredients

2 cups gram flour (*besan*)
¾ cup wholewheat flour (*atta*)
¼ cup fresh coriander leaves, chopped
4 green chillies, chopped
1 medium onion, chopped
1 teaspoon turmeric powder
salt to taste
1 teaspoon *chaat masala*
1 tablespoon pomegranate seeds (*anardana*)
1 tablespoon oil + for greasing
butter to serve.

1 Sift together gram flour and wholewheat flour. Add coriander leaves, green chillies, onion, turmeric powder, salt, *chaat masala*, *anardana* and one tablespoon of oil. Add enough water to make a soft dough. Rest the dough for ten minutes.

2 Divide the dough into sixteen equal portions and shape into balls.

3 Grease your palms with a little oil. Pat each ball of dough between your palms to make a six-inch round *chapati*.

4 Alternatively roll out each ball on a greased and lightly-floured surface with a rolling pin.

5 Cook the *chapati* on a hot *tawa* till done. Spread with butter immediately and serve hot.

CHEF'S TIP

You can also cook Missi *Roti* in a hot *tandoor*. Sprinkle water on one side of the *chapati* and stick it onto the inner wall of the *tandoor*.

Mughlai Parantha

Ingredients

1½ cups refined flour (*maida*)+ for dusting
1½ cups wholewheat flour (*atta*)
¼ cup semolina (*rawa*)
salt to taste
6 tablespoons *ghee* + for shallow frying
½ cup milk

1 Mix refined flour, wholewheat flour and semolina. Add salt, two tablespoons of *ghee* and milk and knead into a stiff dough. Cover and leave to rest for thirty minutes.

2 Divide dough into eight equal portions; roll in refined flour and rest again for ten minutes. Roll out each portion into a thin *chapati* and spread with *ghee*. Dust with some flour and fold in half. Spread a little more *ghee*, dust with flour and once again fold lengthways in half.

3 Stretch the dough and roll up into a spiral and then roll once again into a ball. Press lightly with your fingers and roll out into a *parantha*.

4 Heat a *tawa* and place the *parantha* on it. Turn over after a minute and spread *ghee* on the cooked side. Turn again and spread *ghee* on the other side too. Shallow-fry till both sides are cooked and golden. Crush lightly between the palms of your hands to separate the layers and serve.

Varqi Parantha

Ingredients

4 cups refined flour (*maida*)
1 cup milk
2½ teaspoons sugar
salt to taste
¾ cup pure *ghee* + for shallow-frying

1. Warm milk slightly and dissolve sugar in it.

2. Sift flour with salt. Make a well in the centre of the flour; pour in the milk and about a half cup of water. Mix into the flour gradually and knead into a soft dough. Cover with a damp cloth and set aside for ten minutes.

3. Melt *ghee* and add two-thirds of it to the dough, incorporating it gradually; knead again. Cover the dough and set aside for ten minutes. Place the dough on a lightly-floured surface and roll out into a rectangle.

4. Apply one-fourth of the remaining *ghee* evenly over the rolled dough, dust with flour, fold one end over two-third of the

rectangle, and then fold the other end over it to make three folds. Cover and refrigerate for ten minutes. Repeat this process thrice.

5 Roll the dough into a one-eighth inch thick rectangle and cut out four-inch circles with a cutter. Make three crisscross evenly spaced incisions on the surface of each *parantha*.

6 Place the *paranthas* on sheets of greaseproof paper and refrigerate until ready to cook.

7 Heat a *tawa*; add *ghee* and shallow-fry *paranthas* over low heat until golden brown on both sides. Serve immediately.

CHEF'S TIP

The longer you refrigerate the dough, the flakier the *paranthas*. However do not refrigerate the dough for more than eight hours.

Methi Parantha

Ingredients

1 cup wholewheat flour (*atta*)
1 cup chopped fenugreek leaves (methi)
½ cup gram flour (*besan*)
salt to taste
1 teaspoon red chilli powder
3 tablespoons *ghee*
½ cup yogurt
½ ripe banana, peeled and mashed
4 tablespoons oil

1. Sift together *atta*, *besan,* salt and red chilli powder.

2. Add chopped *methi* leaves, *ghee* and yogurt and mix well. Add mashed banana, two tablespoons of oil and knead into a stiff dough. Cover with a damp cloth and set aside for twenty minutes.

3. Divide the dough into eight equal portions and roll each one out into a five-inch round.

4. Cook on a hot *tawa*, brushing both sides with a little oil, till cooked and light golden brown.

CHEF'S TIP

Methi parantha does not need any water and can stay fresh for three or four days.

Naan

Ingredients

- 4 cups refined flour (*maida*)
- 1 teaspoon baking powder
- ½ teaspoon soda bicarbonate
- 1 teaspoon salt
- 2 teaspoons sugar
- 1 egg (optional)
- 1 cup milk
- 2 tablespoons yogurt
- 2 teaspoons onion seeds (*kalonji*)
- 12 tablespoons oil
- 2 teaspoons butter

1. Sift flour together with baking powder, soda bicarbonate and salt. Add sugar, egg, milk, yogurt and water. Knead well into a medium soft dough.
2. Apply a little oil on the dough, cover with a damp cloth and set aside for one hour.
3. Divide the dough into eight equal portions and shape into balls. Apply a little oil on each ball and sprinkle the onion seeds on top.
4. Flatten each ball of dough into a six-inch circle.

5 Stretch the dough on one side to make a triangular shape. Place on a piece of cloth and press onto the wall of a pre-heated *tandoor* or cook in a preheated oven at 200°C/400°F/Gas Mark 6.

6 Remove with the help of skewers when it is crisp and brown on both sides

7 Serve hot, topped with butter.

CHEF'S TIP

You can also make Naans without the egg. The loss of taste and texture will hardly be noticeable.

Sheermal

Ingredients

2 cups refined flour (*maida*)

salt to taste

2 teaspoons sugar

¾ cup + 3 tablespoons warm milk

a few saffron threads

2-3 drops *kewra* essence

¼ cup pure *ghee*

2 tablespoons butter + for greasing

1 Sift refined flour with salt. Dissolve sugar in three-fourth cup of warm milk. Soak saffron in three tablespoons of warm milk.

2 Add the dissolved sugar and the *kewra* essence to the flour; mix well. Add one-eighth cup of water and knead into a soft dough. Cover with a damp cloth and set aside for ten minutes.

3 Melt *ghee* and mix it into the dough. Knead again, cover and set aside for ten more minutes.

4 Divide dough into sixteen equal portions and shape into balls; cover and set aside for ten minutes.

5 Preheat the oven to 240°C/475°F/Gas Mark 9. Flatten the balls on a lightly-floured surface and roll each one out into six-inch rounds. Prick the surface with a fork.

6 Grease a baking tray with butter. Arrange the *sheermals* on it and bake in the preheated oven for five minutes.

7 Remove from the oven, brush with saffron-flavoured milk and bake again for three to four minutes.

8 Brush with butter and serve immediately.

CHEF'S TIP

Resting the dough before rolling it out, helps to moisten and soften it and make it more pliable.

Peethiwali Poori

Ingredients

1½ cups wholewheat flour (*atta*)
¼ cup split black gram (*dhuli urad dal*)
salt to taste
1 tablespoon oil + for deep-frying
3 tablespoons *ghee*
a pinch of asafoetida (*hing*)
1½ teaspoons cumin seeds
2 tablespoons coriander seeds
1 teaspoon red chilli powder
1 inch cinnamon
sea salt to taste

1. Wash and soak *dhuli urad dal* in one cup of water for two hours.
2. Mix *atta*, salt and one tablespoon of oil in a bowl. Add enough water and knead into a dough. Cover with a damp cloth and set aside.
3. For the stuffing, heat *ghee* in a pan. Add asafoetida, cumin seeds and coriander seeds and sauté for a few seconds. Drain the *dal*, add to the pan and sauté for a while. Stir in the red chilli powder.
4. Break the cinnamon into smaller pieces and crush coarsely. Add sea salt and crush again. Add this mixture to the *dal*.

5 Divide the dough into twelve equal portions and roll into balls. Make a hollow in each ball, fill it with the stuffing and shape into a ball again. Press lightly on a tabletop.

6 Shape into *pooris* with your hands or with a rolling pin.

7 Heat oil in a *kadai*; slide the *pooris* gently into the hot oil and deep-fry till the *pooris* puff up and both sides are evenly cooked.

8 Drain on absorbent paper and serve hot.

Rajasthani Baati

Ingredients

2 cups wholewheat flour (*atta*)
¼ teaspoon baking powder
2 teaspoons salt
⅔ cup pure *ghee* + for soaking
½ teaspoon carom seeds (*ajwain*)

1. Sift flour, baking powder and salt together.
2. Rub two-third cup of *ghee* into the flour mixture till it resembles breadcrumbs.
3. Add *ajwain* and approximately three-fourth cup of water and knead into a dough.
4. Preheat an oven to 220°C/425°F/Gas Mark 7.
5. Divide the dough into eight equal portions and shape into balls. Bake for about ten minutes. Lower heat to 200°C/400°F/Gas Mark 6 and continue to bake for thirty to thirty-five minutes more.
6. Remove from the oven, press lightly and soak in a bowl of melted *ghee* for at least one hour or till ready to serve.
7. Serve with *dal* and *ghee*.

Aam Ka Parantha With Chhunda Stuffing

Ingredients

2 cups wholewheat flour (*atta*) + for dusting
salt to taste
½ cup mango pulp
2 tablespoons oil + for deep-frying
1 cup *chhunda*

1 Make a dough with wheat flour, salt, mango pulp and two tablespoons of oil. Divide into eight equal portions.

2 Dust each ball of dough with flour and roll out into a small *roti*. Spread with a little oil and sprinkle with a little flour. Put a tablespoonful of *chhunda* at one end of the *roti* and roll into a cylinder. Fold in the two ends and press lightly. Cover and leave the rolls to rest for a while.

3 Dust each roll with a little flour and gently roll out again into squares. Shake off excess flour.

4 Heat a *tawa*. Place a *parantha* on it and cook both sides on medium heat. Drizzle some oil around the edges and cook till both sides are golden and crisp.

5 Serve hot with *chhunda*.

Tandoori Roti

Ingredients

2 cups refined flour (*maida*)
salt to taste

1 Sift flour and salt into a bowl.

2 Add enough water and knead into a soft, smooth dough. Cover with a damp cloth and set aside for a few minutes. Divide the dough into four equal portions.

3 Pat each ball on the palm of your hand, till approximately five or six inches in diameter.

4 Stick it onto the inner wall of a moderately hot *tandoor*. Remove when cooked. Serve hot.

5 Alternatively, cook *tandoori rotis* in an oven. Place *rotis* on a greased baking tray and cook for five or six minutes at 190°C/375°F/Gas Mark 5.

Rice Bhakri

Ingredients

2 cups + ¼ cup rice flour
salt to taste
sesame seeds (*til*) as required

1. Sift together two cups of rice flour and salt. Add enough warm water to make a soft dough.
2. Divide the dough into four portions and shape into balls.
3. Dust a *thali* or a table top with a little rice flour. Flatten each portion of the dough with your palm into a moderately thick *bhakri*.
4. Heat a *tawa* till moderately hot and place a *bhakri* on it.
5. Brush the top of the *bhakri* with water while it is cooking; turn it over and cook the other side as well, brushing the top with water.
6. When almost cooked, sprinkle *til* seeds on top. The *bhakri* should be soft and fluffy.